EXTREME!

Surviving in the World's Most Extreme Places

Ross Piper

Capstone press

Mankato, Minnesota

Fact Finders is published by Capstone Press,
a Capstone Publishers company.
151 Good Counsel Drive, P.O. Box 669,
Mankato, Minnesota 56002.
www.capstonepress.com

First published 2009

Library of Congress Cataloging-in-Publication Data

Piper, Ross.
  Surviving in the world's most extreme places / by Ross
Piper.
  p. cm. -- (Fact finders. Extreme explorations!)
  ISBN 978-1-4296-4560-7
  ISBN 978-1-4296-4623-9 (pbk.)
  1. Animals--Adaptation--Juvenile literature. 2. Extreme
environments--Juvenile literature. I. Title. II. Series.

QL49.P575 2010
591.4--dc22

2009028662

Produced for A & C Black by
MONKEY PUZZLE MEDIA LTD
Monkey Puzzle Media Ltd
48 York Avenue
Hove BN3 1PJ, UK

Editor: Susie Brooks
Design: Mayer Media Ltd
Picture research: Lynda Lines
Series consultants: Jane Turner and James de Winter

This book is produced using paper that is made from
wood grown in managed, sustainable forests. It is natural,
renewable, and recyclable. The logging and manufacturing
processes conform to the environmental regulations of the
country of origin.

Printed in Malaysia by Tien Wah Press (Pte.) Ltd

102009
005558

Picture acknowledgements
Corbis pp. 5 (Ralph White), 24 (Lynsey Addario), 28;
Paul Cziko pp. 6–7; FLPA pp. 6 (Konrad Wothe/ Minden
Pictures), 8 (Frans Lanting), 8–9 (Michael and Patricia
Fogden), 10–11 (Flip Nicklin/Minden Pictures); Getty
Images pp. 16 (Peter David), 24–25 (Pankaj and Insy
Shah), 27 top (Dr. T. J. Beveridge); iStockphoto pp.
20–21 (James Richey); Monterey Bay Aquarium Research
Institute pp. 22–23; Natural History Museum, London p.
23; Nature Picture Library pp. 14 (Fred Olivier), 15 (Fred
Olivier), 26–27 (George McCarthy), 28–29 (David Tipling);
Photolibrary.com p. 19 (Marevision); Rex Features pp.
1 (Nature Picture Library), 10 (Nature Picture Library),
16–17 (Nature Picture Library); Science Photo Library
pp. 12 (Andrew Syred), 12–13 (Steve Gschmeissner), 18
(Dr. Ken Macdonald), 20 (T-Service); Topfoto.co.uk p. 4.

The front cover shows emperor penguin chicks huddled
together for warmth during a snowstorm in Antarctica
(Nature Picture Library/Fred Olivier).

Every effort has been made to contact copyright holders
of material reproduced in this book. Any omissions will
be rectified in subsequent printings if notice is given to the
publishers.

CONTENTS

Life is tough   4
Dicing with ice   6
Rain drain   8
Super diver   10
The living dead   12
Deep freeze   14
Crushing depths   16
Red-hot worms   18
Bear-ing the cold   20
Bone eaters   22
Desert travelers   24
Taking the heat   26
Using our heads   28
Glossary   30
Further information   31
Index   32

Abbreviations m stands for meters • **ft** stands for feet • **in** stands for inches • **cm** stands for centimeters • **km/h** stands for kilometers per hour • **mph** stands for miles per hour • **°C** stands for Centigrade • **°F** stands for Fahrenheit

Life is tough

Imagine living somewhere that's always dark . . . or scorching hot . . . or icy cold. What if you couldn't find water or had to go for months without food? Sounds tough? Welcome to the world of extreme survivors!

Watery world

About 70 percent of Earth's surface is covered by ocean. More than 50 percent of this water is over 2 miles (3 kilometers) deep. Down there is a place for serious survivors.

Amazingly, much of Earth's surface makes it difficult for life to survive. In some places there are extreme temperatures, from -128°F (-89°C) in Antarctica to almost 140°F (60°C) in North Africa. In the thirsty deserts of Chile, rain hasn't fallen for at least four hundred years. Meanwhile, deep underwater in the oceans, the **pressure** is enough to crush most animals to death.

Life in Asia's Gobi Desert is certainly extreme. There is very little water, violent storms whirl around, and it's either burning hot or freezing cold. No problem—if you're a camel.

pressure a measure of the amount of force acting on something

Weight from all the water above creates huge pressure.

People can survive down here only inside a specially designed vehicle.

A bait cage lures fish close to the vehicle to be studied.

A **submersible** explores the deep ocean. At 0.6 miles (1 kilometer) down, it is bitterly cold, there is no light, and the pressure is about 100 times that at the surface.

Rat-tail fish have a strong sense of smell to sniff out food in the pitch dark.

submersible a small submarine for exploring and working underwater

Dicing with ice

If you jumped into the water around the North or South Pole, you'd die of cold in minutes. But lots of fish live there and get away with it. What makes them so special?

Blood, like water, can freeze. If a tiny ice crystal gets into the blood of a polar fish through a tiny cut, it grows very quickly. Soon the blood freezes solid, meaning certain death—unless you are an icefish or toothfish. These creatures stay safe thanks to **antifreeze** chemicals in their blood, which stop the ice crystals from growing.

Salt lowers the freezing point of seawater to about 28°F (-2°C)— that's 4°F (2°C) colder than fresh water. Close up, you can see the water turning into ice crystals.

antifreeze a substance that lowers a liquid's freezing point

The toothfish swims slowly to save energy.

Frozen frog

During the winter, the common wood frog freezes solid! When the weather warms up again in spring, the frog **thaws** out and feels just fine.

Hello, fish face!

Fish's heart beats just once every six seconds.

Large eyes help the fish to see in the dark, polar waters.

An Antarctic toothfish swims around in search of smaller fish to eat.

thaw to melt or defrost

Rain drain

Deserts can be very hot and very dry. They're just the kinds of places to bake an unfortunate frog to a crisp— or so you might think.

A desert rain frog peeps out of its hole. If there is no rain, rain frogs can stay buried in the sand for years.

Soggy froggy

The water-holding frog of Australia also survives by hiding underground. Aboriginal people dig it up and squeeze it to get a drink of clean water.

Desert rain frogs can survive in some of the driest places on Earth. For most of the year, they shelter from the scorching heat by burying themselves in the sand. When there's a rainy spell, the frogs pop out. They feed, mate and lay their eggs in a couple of weeks. Then, when it gets too hot and dry again, they burrow back down.

estivation a deep sleeplike state, similar to hibernation

This desert rain frog is sampling life out in the open. He doesn't look too happy about it!

Soaked again!

The body can hold a lot of water to be used when the frog is underground.

The frog has strong limbs for digging its burrow.

Once buried, the frog enters a long **estivation**.

Under the ground, the frog sheds skin to form a **cocoon**.

cocoon a protective covering

Super diver

How long can you hold your breath underwater? One minute? Two minutes at most. The sperm whale can hold its breath for about two hours!

Sperm whales are massive creatures that hold the world diving record. They can dive to depths of at least 10,000 feet (3,000 meters)—that's 10 Eiffel towers piled on top of each other!

It's very dark down there, so the whales hunt using sound. They send out a noise and wait until it bounces back off their **prey**. This is called echolocation.

An exhausted sperm whale brings its giant squid dinner to the surface— and takes a well-earned breath.

prey animals that are hunted by other animals for food

A diver looks tiny next to the huge sperm whale. Male sperm whales can grow up to 60 ft (20 m) long and have the largest heads of any animal.

Record breaker

The sperm whale isn't just the world's best diver. It also has the thickest skin and the biggest brain, which is about nine times bigger than yours!

1 Sperm whale breathes air at the surface through a blowhole in its head.

2 **Oxygen** from the air enters the whale's blood through its lungs.

3 Whale's muscles act like sponges, **absorbing** the oxygen.

4 Muscles use stored oxygen during long dives.

absorb to take in or soak up   **oxygen** the gas in air that humans and animals need to survive

The living dead

Water bears are such tiny animals that you need a microscope to see them. But what they lack in size, they more than make up for in toughness!

Water bears live in the thin film of water that sticks to land plants, such as mosses. This **habitat** dries out regularly. To survive, the bears lose most of the water from their body and enter into a deathlike state.

In this state, water bears can survive being cooked, deep-frozen, and the conditions in outer space. Next time it rains, they come alive again.

*In its deathlike state, a water bear dries out completely. All the water **molecules** in its body are replaced by sugar, which keeps the bear alive.*

A water bear looks like this when times are good.

habitat the natural surroundings of an animal or plant

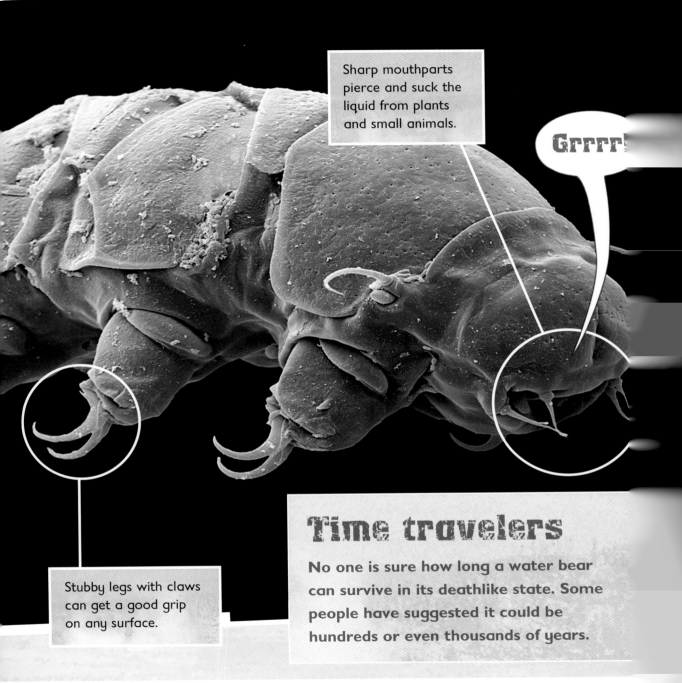

Sharp mouthparts pierce and suck the liquid from plants and small animals.

Grrrr

Stubby legs with claws can get a good grip on any surface.

Time travelers

No one is sure how long a water bear can survive in its deathlike state. Some people have suggested it could be hundreds or even thousands of years.

molecules really tiny groups of linked particles known as atoms

Deep freeze

Most animals try to find somewhere warm and cozy to rear their babies. But not emperor penguins—they seek out the coldest places on Earth.

Emperor penguins go to extraordinary efforts to breed and lay their eggs. To find the perfect spot, they slide and shuffle for about 75 miles (120 kilometers) across the Antarctic ice. The female lays a single egg, then leaves her mate and trudges all the way back to the ocean. Meanwhile, the male is left to care for the egg for two months of bitter cold and no food.

*Male penguins form tight huddles to **conserve** heat. The huddle shuffles round slowly so that every penguin gets a turn in the snug center.*

conserve to use something sparingly or make it last   **blubber** a thick layer of fat

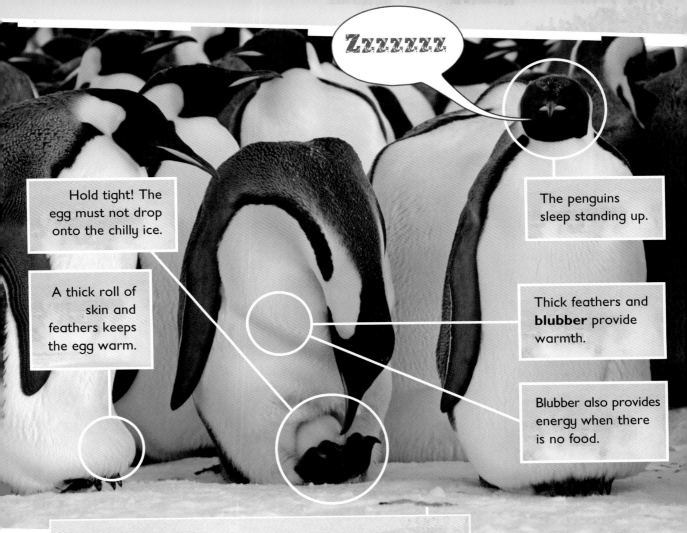

Zzzzzzz

Hold tight! The egg must not drop onto the chilly ice.

A thick roll of skin and feathers keeps the egg warm.

The penguins sleep standing up.

Thick feathers and **blubber** provide warmth.

Blubber also provides energy when there is no food.

Toasty toes

If you stood on the Antarctic ice in your bare feet, they'd go blue in minutes. Penguins don't get **frostbite** because warm blood flowing around their body heats the cold blood coming from their feet.

The male penguin keeps the egg safe by balancing it on his feet. He must look after it until it hatches and then his mate will return to feed the chick.

frostbite damage to body parts such as toes and fingers, due to extreme cold

Crushing depths

Fish from the deep ocean look like creatures from a nightmare. You might think they're living in a nightmare, too. Real-life habitats don't come much tougher than theirs.

The deep sea covers more of Earth than any other habitat. But life down there is harsh. There is no light, and it's really cold. The pressure from all the water above is enormous and there's very little food. Still, fish manage to live in this dark, scary place. They've found some pretty extreme ways of surviving—as you can see from these anglerfish.

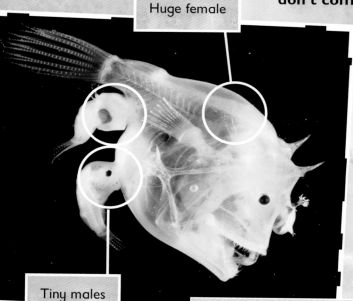

Huge female

Tiny males

It's hard to find a mate when you're an anglerfish. Once the males have spied a female, they bite her and won't let go.

Mate for life

While the tiny male anglerfish clings to the female, he gets nutrients from her body. Slowly his flesh melts into hers, until he's just a part of his giant mate.

nutrients the things in food that all life needs to grow and be healthy

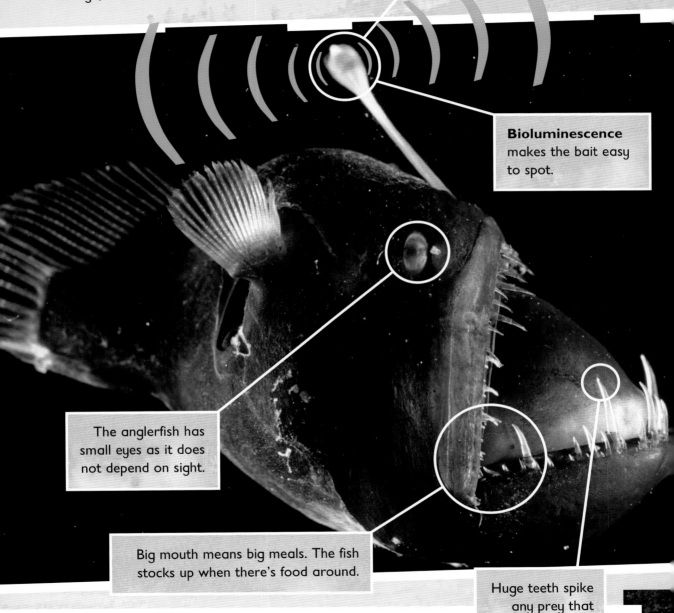

A female deep-sea anglerfish is not much bigger than an orange, with an enormous mouth for her size.

Fleshy growth from the fish's head acts as a bait to attract prey.

Bioluminescence makes the bait easy to spot.

The anglerfish has small eyes as it does not depend on sight.

Big mouth means big meals. The fish stocks up when there's food around.

Huge teeth spike any prey that swims up close.

bioluminescence   light produced naturally by some living things

Red-hot worms

At the bottom of the ocean, life breaks all the rules. The weird creatures that live here will never see sunlight. What's more, they can survive in super-hot water full of deadly gases.

Scorching water gushes from a "black smoker" vent in the seafloor.

In some parts of the seabed, **magma** super-heats water to scorching temperatures. The water gushes out of cracks and crevices, eventually forming chimneylike holes called vents. Spurting out with the water are lots of poisonous gases. These would kill most animals in seconds—but they're nothing to the giant tube worm. In fact, they keep this colorful creature alive.

Life's beginnings

Some scientists believe these deep-sea vents are where life first began—at least 3 billion years ago.

magma super-hot, molten rock found inside Earth

Giant tube worms cluster around a vent of magma-heated water.

Gases make their way to bacteria deep inside the worm.

Worms live on the nutrients **bacteria** produce.

Featherlike tops absorb the gases.

Worm bodies are as big as your wrist.

Each worm lives inside a tough tube.

bacteria tiny, single-celled living things

Bear-ing the cold

Polar bears may look soft and cuddly, but beware. They are actually fearsome beasts, fighting to survive in one of the most punishing places on the planet.

Dark areas are giving off the most heat.

Life in the Arctic is no joke. In the winter there is hardly any sunlight, and it rarely gets warmer than -40°F (-40°C). Howling winds stir up snow and force the temperature even lower.

Most animals would drop down dead in this giant deep freeze but, remarkably, the polar bear is quite at home. This huge, snow-white animal has lots of special features to help it survive the cold.

*This picture, called a **thermogram**, shows that the polar bear loses very little heat. Most of its surface is the same temperature as the snow, meaning its body warmth is snugly trapped inside.*

thermogram a picture from a heat-sensitive camera   **adapt** change to suit the surroundings

20

Seal or walrus for dinner today? Polar bears are fierce hunters and powerful swimmers, too.

Cold lover

The polar bear is so well **adapted** to the cold that it starts to overheat if the temperature rises above 50°F (10°C). Even running around can be too much for this chilled-out creature.

Underneath the skin is a 4-in (10-cm) layer of blubber for **insulation**.

Nice warm day!

An extra, see-through eyelid protects the eye from bright light reflected off the snow.

Fur is thick and waterproof.

Big feet with tiny lumps on their soles give good grip on the snow and ice.

insulation something that stops heat from escaping

21

Bone eaters

What happens to a dead whale? Its body sinks to the ocean floor and becomes a feast for thousands of animals. Not even the bones will go to waste.

When a whale dies, its **corpse** eventually settles on the seabed. Here, a mass of worms, fish, snails and crabs feed on the flesh until there is nothing left but a skeleton. That's when the zombie worm appears!

The zombie worm loves skeletons. It sticks onto the bones and grows into them. Then it uses bacteria to digest the nutritious **marrow** inside.

Many mini-mates

Male zombie worms are very tiny and live inside the female. One female was discovered with 111 males living inside her!

Scientists from the Monterey Bay Aquarium Research Institute in California discovered this whale skeleton on the deep seabed. The pink tufts are female zombie worms, tucking into the bones.

corpse a dead body   **marrow** a soft, fatty substance that is found inside some bones

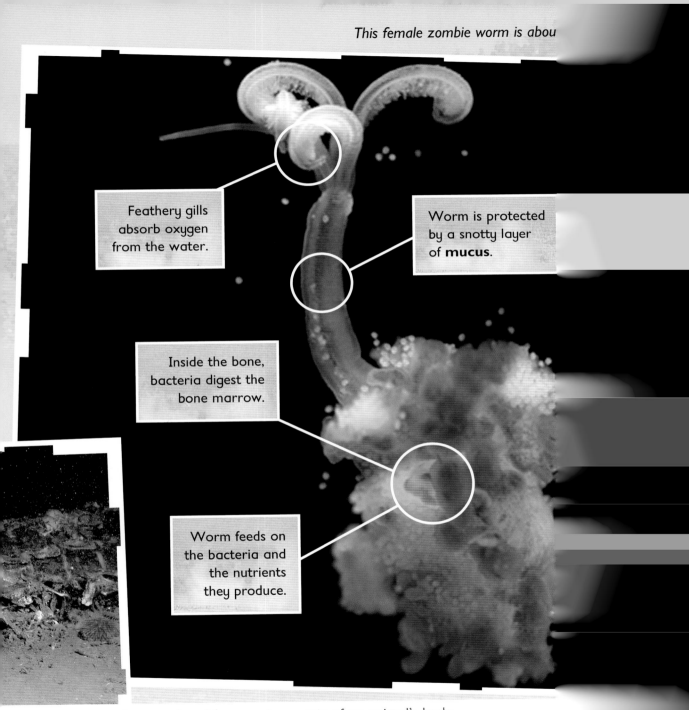

Feathery gills absorb oxygen from the water.

Worm is protected by a snotty layer of **mucus**.

Inside the bone, bacteria digest the bone marrow.

Worm feeds on the bacteria and the nutrients they produce.

mucus a slime produced from various parts of an animal's body

Desert travelers

Feeling thirsty? You could probably survive without water for about three days. A camel, on the other hand, can last for two weeks! These animals may not be much to look at, but they are masters of desert survival.

Sandstorms are one reason why the desert is such a harsh habitat.

Camels are perfectly happy in places that are really hot and dry. They have amazing ways of coping with the sun, sand, and lack of water. They don't even mind going without food for a while.

Camels are so tough that humans have used them for centuries as desert transport. Even today, they are better than a car in some areas—if you don't mind an uncomfortable ride!

sandstorm a strong windstorm that carries blinding clouds of sand or dust

Camels can walk on sand without sinking, thanks to their big, flat feet.

Nostrils can shut to keep sand out.

Long eyelashes block out sun, sand, and flies.

Prized dung

In many places, people use camel dung instead of wood on fires. They collect the dung and dry it, before burning the stinky stuff.

Hump contains fat.

A camel can drink about 176 pints (100 liters) of water at a time!

Stomach lining stores water.

Fat breaks down inside the body to produce water and energy.

Taking the heat

Bacteria are the oldest life forms on Earth. They are not animals—but they are true survivors. Anywhere that's too hot, too cold, or too acidic for animals to live in, bacteria get on fine.

These bacterial colonies grow very large because there's nothing to eat them.

Bacteria coat the rocks in colorful **biofilms**.

The bacteria survive on gases dissolved in the hot water.

The water is super-heated by magma deep underground.

acidic   containing acid, a sour chemical that can be harmful

Super spores

If conditions become unsuitable, bacteria turn into spores. These can survive just about anything. When conditions are suitable again, the bacteria spring back to life.

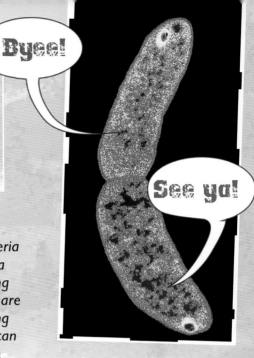

This bacterium from a hot water pool is splitting into two separate cells.

Colonies of colorful bacteria brighten up a pool of boiling water. They are the only living things that can survive here.

Bacteria are too small to see with the naked eye, but they are all around us. They cluster in some surprisingly extreme spots, too. Huge, rainbow-colored colonies of bacteria can be found in pools of scalding water. Meanwhile, thousands of feet underground, other bacteria are nibbling away at rock.

It's hard to find a place where these tiny organisms can't survive.

biofilm a thin slime that bacteria make to help them cling to surfaces

Using our heads

Humans are soft and weak. We like to be warm and dry. Fortunately, our big brains have come up with ways of surviving almost anything.

Humans use brainpower to find ways of coping in **hostile** environments. We know how to keep cool in hot places, and how to warm up in the coldest corners of Earth. One of the hardest places to survive is way beyond our planet, in space. Yet people have found out how to reach space— and stay alive.

An astronaut leaves his spacecraft on a space walk. Without his protective spacesuit, he would be dead in seconds.

hostile unfriendly or difficult to live in

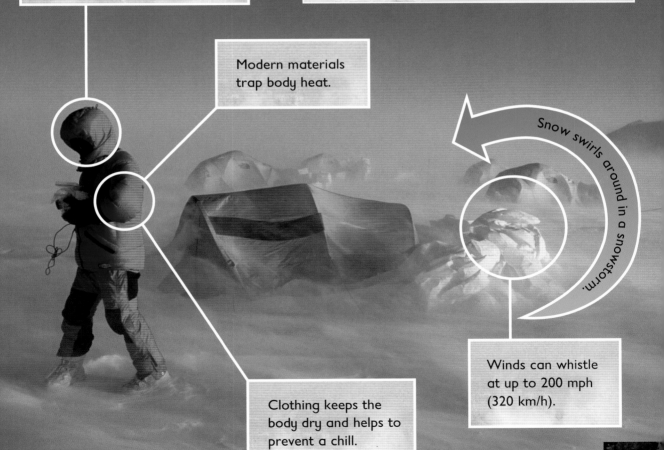

The temperature here in Antarctica can dip as low as -130°F (-90°C). That's nearly five times colder than your freezer!

Surviving death!

Some people have paid lots of money to have their bodies frozen in liquid nitrogen, at -321°F (-196°C), when they die. They hope that one day scientists will find a way to bring them back to life.

Your head loses more heat than any other body part, so it needs good insulation.

Modern materials trap body heat.

Snow swirls around in a snowstorm.

Clothing keeps the body dry and helps to prevent a chill.

Winds can whistle at up to 200 mph (320 km/h).

Glossary

absorb to take in or soak up

acidic containing acid, a sour chemical that can be harmful

adapt change to suit the surroundings

antifreeze a substance that lowers a liquid's freezing point

bacteria tiny, single-celled living things

biofilm a thin slime that bacteria make to help them cling to surfaces

bioluminescence light produced naturally by some living things

blubber a thick layer of fat

cocoon a protective covering

conserve to use something sparingly or make it last

corpse a dead body

estivation a deep sleeplike state, similar to hibernation

frostbite damage to body parts such as toes and fingers, due to extreme cold

habitat the natural surroundings of an animal or plant

hostile unfriendly or difficult to live in

insulation something that stops heat from escaping

magma super-hot, molten rock found inside Earth

marrow a soft, fatty substance that is found inside some bones

molecules really tiny groups of linked particles known as atoms

mucus a slime produced from various parts of an animal's body

nutrients the things in food that all life needs to grow and be healthy

oxygen the gas in air that humans and animals need to survive

pressure a measure of the amount of force acting on something

prey animals that are hunted by other animals for food

sandstorm a strong windstorm that carries blinding clouds of sand or dust

submersible a small submarine for exploring and working underwater

thaw to melt or defrost

thermogram a picture from a heat-sensitive camera

Further information

Books

Extreme Animals: The Toughest Creatures on Earth by Nicola Davies (Walker Books, 2006)
This book illustrates some tough survivors with cartoons.

Animal Planet: The Most Extreme Animals by the Discovery Channel (Jossey-Bass, 2007)
A collection of extreme animals, based on creatures featured on the Discovery Channel.

Extraordinary Animals: An Encyclopedia of Curious and Unusual Animals by Ross Piper (Westport, 2007)
All sorts of weird and wonderful animals, with information on how to find some of them.

Extreme Animals by Steve Parker (Carlton Books Ltd, 2008)
Lots of amazing creatures can be seen in this book.

Web sites

FactHound offers a safe, fun way to find Internet sites related to this book. All of the sites on FactHound have been researched by our staff. Visit *www.facthound.com* for age-appropriate sites. You may browse subjects by clicking on letters, or by clicking on pictures and words.
FactHound will fetch the best sites for you!

Films

Life in the Undergrowth narrated by David Attenborough (BBC Warner, 2005)
Includes brilliant views of smaller animals eating and being eaten, with excellent scenes showing parasites going about their lives.

The Blue Planet narrated by David Attenborough (BBC Video, 2002)
Explores seas and oceans around the world, showing some of Earth's most powerful predators.

Planet Earth narrated by David Attenborough (BBC, Discovery Channel and NHK, 2006)
Earth's habitats and the life they support are seen in great detail in this brilliant series.

Index

anglerfish 16–17

bacteria 19, 22, 23, 26, 27
black smokers 18
blood 6, 7, 11, 15
blubber 15, 21

camels 4, 24, 25
cold 4
    Antarctica 4, 6, 14
    bacteria 26
    deep ocean 5, 16
    polar bears 20, 21

darkness 4, 5, 7, 10, 16
deep ocean 4, 5, 16, 17,
    18, 22
deserts 4, 8, 24
diving 10, 11

echolocation 10
emperor penguins 14–15
energy 7, 15, 25

feathers 15
fish 5, 6, 7, 16, 17, 22
frogs 7, 8–9
fur 21

gases 18, 19, 26
giant tube worms 18, 19

habitats 12, 16, 24
heat 4
    conserving 14, 15, 20,
    21, 29
    deserts 8
    humans 29
    super-heated water 18,
    19, 26, 27

ice 6, 14, 15, 21
icefish 6
insulation 21, 29

nutrients 16, 19, 23

oceans 4, 5, 16, 18, 22
oxygen 11, 23

polar bears 20–21
pressure 4, 5, 16

sand 8, 24, 25
snow 20, 21, 29
space 28
sperm whales 10–11

toothfish 6, 7

water
    deep ocean 4, 5, 22
    lack of 4, 8, 9, 12, 24,
    25
    super-heated 18, 19,
    26, 27
water bears 12–13
whales 10–11, 22
worms 18–19, 22–23